Rise

A. Van Jordan

Tia Chucha Press
Chicago and Los Angeles

ACKNOWLEDGMENTS

Grateful acknowledgment is made to the editors of the following magazines, in which some of the poems herein first appeared. *Arkansas Review* "The Lifestory of Eddie James 'Son' House, Jr., As Told Through His Hands," "The Devil Clears His Name of Rumors Surrounding the Death of Robert L. Johnson," and "The Absence of R.L. Burnside at New York's Autumn Mississippi Blues Festival." *Barrow Street:* "The Journey of Henry 'Box' Brown." *Brilliant Corners:* "Jookin." *Calaloo:* "Rise." *Icarus:* "A Woman from the Projects," "Jookin'" (original version). *North American Review:* "Notes from a Southpaw." *River Oak Review:* "A Debt is Paid." *Seneca Review:* "J.J. Johnson Changes Tempo," "After 75 Years, Greenwood, Oklahoma, Gets A Statue." *Squaw Review:* "Silent Partner." *Warpland:* "Tamara's Dance."

Appreciation also to Kevin James, who composed music for many of these poems, which was published by ASCAP and performed under the title *Jookin*.

"The Journey of Henry 'Box' Brown" won the 1999 Hughes, Diop, Knight Award through the Gwendolyn Brooks Center, Chicago, Illinois.

"The Lifestory of Eddie James Son House Jr., As Told Through His Hands" also appears in *Ravishing DisUnities: Real Ghazals in English,* edited by Agha Shahid Ali, published by Wesleyan University Press, 2000.

"A Debt Is Paid" also appears in *Beyond the Frontier: An Anthology of Contemporary African American Poetry,* edited by E. Ethelbert Miller, published by Black Classics Press.

Appreciation is also given to Warren Wilson College and the MFA Program for Writers for the 1999-2000 Joan Beebe Graduate Teaching Fellowship, during which many of these poems were completed.

Published by Tia Chucha Press
Luis Rodriguez, Founder and Editorial Director

FOR INFORMATION WRITE TO:
Tia Chucha Press
The Guild Complex
1212 N. Ashland, Suite 211
Chicago IL 60622

Distributed by Northwestern University Press.
For orders, call 1 800 621 2736.

The Guild Complex publishes this book with the much appreciated financial support of the Richard H. Driehaus Foundation, the National Endowment for the Arts, the Illinois Arts Council, the John D. and Catherine T. MacArthur Foundation, the WPWR-TV Channel 50 Foundation, the Sara Lee Foundation, and other donors.

Special thanks for support by a grant from the Greenwall Fund of The Academy of American Poets.

Contents

PART 3: PIANOFORTE

PART 4: RISE

for my family

. . .

Also, many thanks to those who kept shining the light:
E. Ethelbert Miller, Cornelius Eady, Claudia Rankine, Agha Shahid Ali,
Eleanor Wilner, Carl Phillips, Laure-Anne Bosselaar, Marita Golden,
Reginald Gibbons and Michael Collier.

Now will I rise, saith the Lord; now will I be exalted;
now will I lift up myself.

—Isaiah 33:10

. . . bind me with your vast arms to the luminous clay
    bind my black vibration to the very navel of the world
    bind, bind me, bitter brotherhood
    then, strangling me with your lasso of stars
    rise,
    Dove
    rise
    rise
    rise. . . .

—Aimé Césaire from
Notebook of a Return to the Native Land

Notes from a Southpaw

Date: Monday, March 25, 1996,
just another day in DC,
and I drink with a friend

in Georgetown, after work.
I'm killing a couple of hours
before I hear Toni Morrison deliver

her Jefferson Lecture at the Kennedy Center.
Inside the Crossing Guard bar,
the white bartender and all his white

patrons watch the afterglow of OJ's
civil case. A white guy in a gray suit
sidles up next to me;

he holds his drink in his left,
a cigarette in his right.
The TV switches, now,

to news of the AIDS-related death
of rapper Easy E. My friend
is not white, Iranian, and I'm the only black

in this bar in Chocolate City.
The guy sitting next to me
says he's tired of these *niggers*

like OJ, tired of rappers using the word
"motherfucker." He says how would
they like to hear me call them all *niggers*.

His words are blurring, there's static and then distinctly,
again, *Nigger*. My friend now tries to capture me
in the spiral of his large, Persian eyes; he hopes

I didn't hear the guy, but he knows me better than this.
Listen, I say, *why don't you take that shit somewhere else?*
He says, *I'm not calling you a nigger unless you feel like one.*

Note: Try not to feel
like one when white people call you this word. Remember history.
Don't give power to the word. I don't want him to think

I am everything he thinks I am. Does that make sense?
Everytime someone black makes the 11:00 news,
someone white says, *See. That's the problem.*

And then I walk into a bar in Georgetown, see?
Question: What would Poitier do
in a situation like this?

What does a man say, when he doesn't want to   erupt,
but still wants to act like a man? I say, *You just shouldn't be so cavalier
about throwing around that word.*

So the guy picks up his bar stool, holds it over his shoulder
like a baseball bat, tells me to *say something else,*
asks me—in a way that's not really a question—if

I *want some of this.* I'm still cool. I tell him
I don't want any trouble. That's right, he says,
and sits back down. **Question:** In history, how many men

were called niggers in front of their wives and children
but couldn't do anything about it?
I wonder how many times he's used the word

nigger in his life.
He comments on his victory
to the bartender. The bartender laughs nervously.

Date: April 1972, recess at Schumacher Elementary,
I befriend the only white kid in the school,
even at this age, my other friends

think I'm crazy; they already had that lesson.
I learned mine when I beat him at racing,
and he called me a word I had never heard before;

his folks had already given him *his* lesson, too.
Nigger!
Still bleeds inside my ear.

Date: October 19, 1977.
When I was a boy, I used to fight all the time.
When I boxed at the Y, although I'm right-handed,

I used a southpaw stance. People never knew
what to make of it. I started this because I got beat
once by a guy who really was a southpaw.

I never forgot the surprise and the pain
of getting hit, when I least expected it.
Rushing with a left-handed blur,

which I only saw when he drew it back,
he set me up for the overhand right.
My hands shifted gears,

freckling his face,
the leather grazed and slipped.
Combinate! My trainer prayed, *Combinate!*

But the southpaw cut the ring off
carrying nightfall in each hand.
Note: Always throw   more than   one punch.

I knew I would have to explain to my mother,
a Christian woman—my swollen eyes,
my curiosity with danger,

my mouth, full of crimson—when I got home.
This held me back, this need to explain
to someone who loved me,

why I had to act like an animal, or,
yes, like a nigger. **Note:** It's been nearly 20 years
since I lived in my mother's house.

Now, this white guy here in the suit,
he thinks I forgot
about him as I sip my beer and wait.

I size him up: he's a little bigger than me
but he's also a little older, which means
he probably has more to lose. **Note:**

The one who has more to lose always loses.
I turn to look at him
and he looks at me; for this moment

we could be lovers as easily as enemies.
I throw my beer mug and it explodes in his face.
Beer and blood and niggers and whites

and I'm dancing in the middle of this constellation.
My punches land clean. I'm standing over him now.
He tries to crawl away. It's too late. All that history

that stopped me earlier, now, won't let me stop.
Question: What will he learn from this beating
that I haven't learned from all of my losses?

And when the police get here, tell me,
how do I make them   understand   all of this?

PART 1

A SMALL FLAME
ON THE HORIZON

Vapors of Sidney Bechet

(born May 14, 1897, New Orleans;
died May 14, 1959, Paris)

If he gargles mood in his mouth
leaving options open to the reed,
   time and space lose significance.

Let's call this, the way a sound is born,
   the way a worksong becomes blues,
ragtime becomes a living,
   blows over an ocean and becomes "art."

What can we call wind that picks up
   blue notes with needle and thread,
with reeds of black or brass? What flows into
   the Embassy Club picking up the scent of imported perfume
or a dance hall lifting sawdust and obscenities?

   Call it a "remembering song."
Call it life's crossroads.
   Something more than the whim of wind,
than a love of music in dark crevices
   and foreign tongues. Let dreams travel
on a staff of sixteenth notes, let them rest
   legato, give them stomps, blues, and ballads.

Let the song change like love that's gone crazy,
   baby teeth in a big boy's head,
shoes on a wealthy woman.

   If it gives birth and death on the same day in May,
haunts and hums in Creole and blues,
   if it growls and swishes in your ear
like a lover's promise,
   call it something that measures distance
beyond the reach of roots.

If it's soprano wind through a saxophone,
      swirled first over Sidney's lips,
call it a man who's made up his mind
      to blow something as beautiful
as a jazzman dancing on a compass.

Sitting In on the Set

The crowd is eager to hand him his hat.
But desire ushers the flugelhorn player
From his seat to the stage

Playing riffs with his fingers crossed;
He might as well blow the horn
Through the holes left by the notes he's missing.

His music swims in the room's colors,
Not making the decor any prettier,
In its war of blood and tar;

His bleak tone blares into the blackness
Of hard luck and lights.
Easier to sit in the front row

With your feet propped on stage
Than to play in a room where
Notes are harder to hold than a cheating lover.

As everyone heckles advice,
Somebody tells a fable about
Dignity and the failed attempt.

Ears press against thin air;
Listen! as a man's dream
Dries up and blows embarrassingly

Through the crowd.

The Woman in Romare Bearden's <u>Encore</u>

wears one ear ring, but two ivory bracelets,
distilled in a fashionable moment
that has nothing to do with fashion, but
has everything to do with style,
or with any adjective a woman earns
before her name. Their gaze

fills her with applause;
the diva smiles shyly through
afterglow's possible demise,
with her right hand alighted
above her left breast,
pledging her humility,
and in her swept-to-one-side hair

a rose opens like the sun,
and--behind her--the spotlights
pare away the darkness
like a nimbus.

Although no tears well her eyes—
there's even a smile on her face—
she still looks scared,
like she expected the crowd
to throw something other than
love. This is why

her awkward face enchants:
she doesn't know what to expect.
It's one of those nights:
she can only soak
in acceptance, in the relief
of accomplishment,
because someone in a remote corner
put their hands together; because someone else
whistled praise; every hand, every heart—
in the stark, puzzled world
of this scene—holds the pieces of light together.

St. John Coltrane African Orthodox Church

Maybe it was the practice of practice,
he and Alice in the grocery store
and him fingering keys up and down
the aisles; the magic
of capturing spirit in a whole note,
in a mouthpiece, in *Alabama* like light
bent through a prism into color.
Maybe they figured out his distant
relationship to Lazarus in '56
pushing the stone from in front
of his open bell, bouncing sound
off the east to the west.
It was intangible
the way he raised a soul to intaglio
like a gospel hymn
raises tongues to tones
understood only by the secret
society of the saxophone.
Alice knew the secrets
of the stars and the notes in between,
the power of layin' hands on scales
and the baptism into the void
between chords and back
to bring forth what had not been
before Trane.

It's no surprise to see
the church, with his face stained
in the glass. No questions
surround the choir of saxophones, the con-
gregation's many shades of sound:
not the skin but the sound,
not the verse but the riff,
not the jazz but the spirit.
How is this any different
from heroin churning a man's soul?

If Jesus can turn water into wine
then a junkie can resurrect as a saint.
Maybe you have not come to the altar
with sucker bites from Satan
up and down your arms, taken the fellowship
wherever you could find it, blown
blood through a horn,
shot up with the devil

and felt him ejaculate in your veins.

When man is at his weakest,
faith has a perfect pitch.

After 75 Years, Greenwood, Oklahoma, Gets a Statue

Fate sent Dick Rowland's flat
feet over the tripwire
threshold of an elevator
into the arms of a white woman.
>   The kinda mistake that could
>   get any 19 year old black man hanged;
>   that could give cause for matchheads
>   to dance in Oklahoma heat; that could send
>   black families running into the woods
>   while their homes burn like the voice of God.
"He just stumbled,"
was the final police statement,
but the lynch mob jury already waited
outside where "The Negro
Wall Street of America" would fall
because one man fell.
>   40 city blocks, 23 churches, 400 shops
>   and 600 homes and all black. Can you imagine
>   Rowland's eyes when he fell out
>   of that elevator, when he saw the town
>   burn like a cigarette in a nervous mouth,
when shotguns ushered
black men from the Convention Hall
into the streets,
and out from this world?
>   How do you describe
>   when something goes so terribly wrong?
>   Folks never talk about
>   what they did to the women.
Armstrong's gravelly voice
cannot sing of Greenwood.
The trombone can't even hit
these low notes.
>   The black marble mirrors
>   survivors still holding hats
>   over their hearts,

while children—too young to remember—
play around the feet of the monument.
One child runs past, stops, and bends
down to secure *his* loose shoe lace.

A Debt Is Paid

We younger kids were playing
when Johnny took the stray
dog in his hands,
took a stick,
stuck it in the dog's butt,
broke it off there.

We were just playing
and too afraid to stop
this staged nightmare;
too afraid he'd do
the same to one of us.

Years later, they say,
Johnny owed people.
The news did not surprise me:

he was found naked
hanging like a raw light bulb
from the ceiling of his garage,
body bloated,
hands bound,
a bouquet of credit cards
and dollar bills planted
in his ass. He swung
like that for days till
someone went to see what
the dogs were barking at.

A Bensonhurst Resident Remembers
the Death of Yusuf Hawkins

After years unravel around us,
neighborhoods age like neighbors: windows board up,
shadows grow on corners, posters peel from poles.

New York's Brooklyn borough sprawls
out like a sleepy dog under 90 degree shade;
not hard to imagine: from 1834 to 1898 a city of its own,

until populated with the autumn-colored people
of now, New York city's youngest son
sliced into neighborhoods.

Midtown traffic pauses over the spine of Manhattan
bridge, a steel nerve stretched between the Atlantic
ocean and the inner city.

The slab spans the river between lower Manhattan
and Brooklyn and splinters into Bay Ridge or Flatbush.
But from "Bed-Stuy" to Bensonhurst, flashbacks never change:

> Three black teens travel from Hegeman Ave. to the corner
> of 69th and 20th streets. They encounter our Italian boys,
> who are as sure as a fist,

> as unpredictable as an open hand. On the fringe,
> the women's faces drape like torn clothes.

No, nothing changes—

even years later—even fear in the eyes;
everyone is afraid
to walk across their incision of the city.

It's not that we all carry a piece of Yusuf's
body, his pierced lungs, his open pores,
not even a drop of his blood, no,

we carry the history of our own bodies
spawned from youth. Both camps recall how
the legs moved on oiled pistons,

how the arms threw rocks and bottles,
how the mouth could curse spit-laced words
without a second thought. We remember

talking our way out of trouble,
playing stickball in the middle of the street,
buying our first car. We were simply kids—

after all—kids in the heat
of instinct and ignorance and now
with the life-blood to reminisce on mistakes.

Public Radio Plays Eddie Harris

Clouds stand in protest of morning.

I wonder should I cross this picket-line sky and go to work.

The 70 bus stood me up for our 8:32am date.

Headlines say I voted for a man who cheated on his wife.

By 2:00pm my body's at war with a virus.

I am now blue fire.

My throat is lined with cactus.

There was no mention of this in the morning paper.

I crawl back home to my room; my bedsheets are cold.

At 10:00pm a call of bad news from my family:

Something about a car and my brother.

Doctors say he may never dance again.

This chord of bad news accompanies today's riff.

Folks *have* gone on strike in heaven.

Sweat pours off the shoulders of the night.

No need for liquids and drugs, I'm already dead.

If WPFW FM can't resurrect me, Lazarus was a liar.

Thank God, they're playing Eddie Harris.

I have friends who are atheists.

I have ammunition for our next argument:

They play four Eddie Harris tunes in a row!

Faith healers are tuning in.

I'm all but cured when they make the announcement:

Eddie Harris died today.

Thoughts tornado over my bed.

It pirouettes over the city with hips like my mama's.

Eddie always said there's no such thing as a wrong note,

Only bad connections to the next.

I put the alarm clock under the sheets.

In the morning it will sound like music.

Three Stories of Cotton

1.
In the arid sun,
men stoop to pick cotton bolls
till their backs bleed sweat.

2.
It takes a strong man
to fill a fifty-pound bag
with wind-blown cotton.

3.
A girl faces cruel
wind in a field of cotton.
She bends for no one.

Beggar's Song

I don't remember the last time
I was touched.
In a dream, a tongue —
Or, just breath—
Outlined my navel
With flute music
And I curled up,
Rolled to an empty beach,
Burrowed into wet sand.

When I woke,
My life was full of contradiction.
I trusted no one   not
The one who loved me   not
The ground that held me   not
The sky that caressed my cowling back.

My only fear is love;
I have a defense against all others.
My only friend is my skin;
I send letters to myself.

If I could dream now,
A dark woman would obsess
Over my hands.
She would stalk
Through brush and trees and other earth
To corner me on my back,
Stab me with her tongue,
Dance with all the forbidden steps
That my heart kept secret.

In my life, I've hid from everything above my head.
I knew my life was empty, yet I lived long.
We all come from dust. I rub my belly to the ground.
Every man has a song. I like guitars; they're full of emotion.
We all must die,

But in my death, let me live.
Take my husk and make a *charango*.
Open me up and throw away my armor.
Let blood and tears mingle with music.
Let my naked body be a mirror to the world.
Smell what lack of love does to the flesh.

A *charango* is a South American string instrument made from the shell of an armadillo.

Tamara's Dance

I cannot pin
Point her magic:
The fillip found
In the click of her eyes,
The percussion of her hips,
The apparition possessing her bones
Pirouetting from flamenco
Into jazz into my dreams.
Cigarette smoke writhes to the ceiling,
Like a cobra caught in her spell.
Her shadow struggles to keep up.
Her body, flint; her
Movement, friction; my eyes, fire.
First, the lights are pearl
Then lapis, then they cower
Under the shimmer of legs.
She dances and smoke becomes rain clouds.
She dances and jugular veins beat like bass drums.
She dances as ice cubes spill down spines.
Some mechanical power
Keeps me on her beat, keeps
My mind spinning on her axis,
My eyes transfixed on her dancing.
As lights wash her naked body,
I become a small country
Looking up at my leader.

Sunshine

When I think of the attention men pay to you,
It's as if you've stuck the sun underneath your dress
And every time you walk down the street
Begins the first day of spring. Men say,
Damn baby, you sure lookin' good,
But they don't recognize your beauty.
They don't realize when the weather man said,
70° and sunny skies with a mild westerly breeze,
That he was reading your horoscope.

These are not religious men. They don't know
That God appears in many forms: burning bushes
Or maybe fluorescent flashes of legs on the street
Turning eyes into searchlights. Sometimes,
God is trapped in the fit of spandex,
Which makes men speak in tongues.
Sometimes you pass by them, just in time,
Saving their lives: the tambourine of your heels
In the distance gives them the holy ghost, let alone,
If they looked directly at you:
Their hearts would fold up.
Their lips would crack in your perfumed breeze.
These men—charlatans and gift bearers—
Simply are not willing to kneel at your altar:

If you opened your doors, would they be ready—
Blessed with the gospel music of your voice,
Bathed in your ocean of forgiveness—
For baptism, not by water,
But by the painted toes of the flame behind the light?

Wishbone

Love, and the couples who dance
Around its truth, can be hidden deep
Here in the Hi-Dee-Ho Lounge.
It sits in a red-leather, back-corner booth
Where lovers share the barbecue chicken special
And a pint of Old Crow.
Love grows weightless as the globe,
With its playful candle, burns the mood
To vermilion and plays on their smiles.
The woman licks the meal from his hand,
Gingerly and slow, and then
Their faces meet, just for a breath,
Before he pulls back
And pulls out, from his mouth, a wishbone.
Love can be hidden in the palm of a hand
As the letter Y, picked clean by his lips,
Shimmers now in her eyes;
She shuts them and wraps
Her girlish fingers around the fossil.
He squints hard as if hoisting a beggar's prayer;
As if he thinks he has to lift it by himself.
Their eyes are closed to the world.
They see each other clearly.

The Walkin' Blues

*When you wake up and can't find your shoes, well then
you know you got the walkin' blues.*
                              —Robert L. Johnson

Toes painted by her lover,
   what woman wouldn't feel lucky
walking barefoot over a carpet of two men:
   one unknowing,
one in it for the game?

   When she reaches for her shoes,
it will be only a moment before her husband rattles keys
   at the front door. Her lover must stretch under the bed
for his wingtips before tip-toeing
   out the back.

      *

Down the street, a gambler
   knows better than to misplace his alligators.
He slips his silk-ribbed socks
   off and plants them—and the slim knot of bills
that earlier bulged in his pants—
   in his shoes on top of his dresser.

      *

What's learned from the old man who lives above them
   with the near-winning lottery ticket
and the missing Stacy Adams,
   is that one digit failed him in his fortune,
he should have played his dollar boxed
   or trusted his shoe size
instead of his dream.

*

Next door, a tenor sax
    warms up lips for a set
in between modal chords,
    somewhere between the connection
of E minor to E major in Coltrane's
    My Favorite Things. Tonight, he will hit
all the notes in between the notes.
    Last night, he slept with his shoes on.

Before he steps onto the bandstand
    the woman with the painted toes
will have kissed her husband three times
    standing tall in her high-heel house shoes
reaching up to her man, smiling
    through fresh red lipstick
as if she just slipped her foot,
    easily, into the missing glass slipper.

A Woman from the Projects

Switching down the street
in your summer shorts,
your hips hold memory:
days when your stride demanded
good manners, when sequined dresses
shimmered down your backside.

You step in imagination
of those times. Your saunter still
conjures men. A proud woman
dances beneath your skin.
In this way, time has been your lover.
Your heels still click to the tune
of a man's heartbeat.

On your head, pink rollers
peek from under a scarf.
As you move, I dream
them into a diadem.
Your man must have steel-mill arms
and lumberyard legs to have a woman
who walks with such freedom—
where is he? Embarrassed,

I wonder,
reduced to a sinner,
robbing you of this quiet moment
as you become a small flame on this street's horizon.

PART 2

BLUE HANDS

Cheating Woman Blues Haiku

In whipping noon sun,
a black snake dances through grass
to warm milk in bowls.

In biting noon sun,
a black snake dances through grass
to warm milk in bowls.

Daisies in her hair,
my woman crosses the tracks
to another man.

Cuttin' trees all day,
sweat and sawdust in my eyes;
she thinks I can't see.

Cuttin' trees all day,
sweat and sawdust cloud my eyes;
she thinks I can't see.

In a field of grass,
she lays her head down to dream
of muddy waters.

Jookin'

The joint—raised on stilts, wrapped in ruffled tin,
Hid back in swampland—was a place where,
People say, you could hide from your old lady.
So I slid in hoping that drunken moon could keep a secret.
Armstrong's voice turned black and blue.
Tamara sat on my lap
To whisper prom-night promises she'd only keep
If I kept 'em comin'.
Folks paid us no mind.
Too concerned with coffee pots
Serving liquor into paper cups,
The funk of greens and fish
Drowning tobacco breath and cheap perfume.
A flash of pastel dresses
Blurred on the dance floor:
Blues and yellows became emerald
Women in my blood-shot eyes.
I looked like a child playing with colors till
Vesta walked in,
One hand on her hip
The other in her purse.
I hadn't seen her when folks around us
Moved like bus boys clearing tables.
The smoke in the air stood on its hind legs.
Tamara peeled herself from my lap.
It got so quiet you could hear
A gnat piss on cotton:
The record changed to the B side and
My eyes rolled like
Dice at the feet of my woman.
But I didn't blink until
I washed down the last of my bourbon while
Satchmo finished growling through the jukebox.

The Devil Clears His Name of Rumors Surrounding the Death of Robert L. Johnson

I.
Robert Johnson didn't invent the emotion
That streamed through every song,
That was something his mama taught him about life,
The wail of a grown man when his heart is broken,
The sound of his stepfather coming home
To an empty house, the whisper of his mama
In another man's ear.
I tell you, everybody knew his mother,
Julia Dodd, was livin' wrong.
Shadows would gather behind her and swap stories;
Soiled linen held her secrets;
The mailman read her letters.
I tell you, this is the truth: I knew this woman.

II.
Robert L. put the hope of the homely woman
In a flatted fifth note.
Strummed the gratitude of an older woman
With his fingers.
They were like hotel rooms:
In every town, he collected keys to their homes.
When you saw him stepping sideways to a gal
That was not his voice you heard;
That was his mama,
Whispering in his soul.
All he had to do was repeat the words
His mother never heard.
Let me make it plain:
A night passes filled with lies.
In the morning, the crops are still waiting
For the man who survives the night.
It takes little effort to put a hand behind a woman's head
When kissing her deeply.

How hard is it to play the blues
On a woman's body?
What does a blues man have to lose?
His stepfather called him "no 'count" cause he was gettin' behind
Women and guitars instead of mules and crops.
But let's face it: The boy had talent.

III.
When Robert strummed his guitar, his mama was there too.
Some said, *"The devil must be hidin' out on the roof,*
playin' another guitar,"
Loaning him a third hand.

When he returned to his teachers—playing better than their dreams,
His guitar tuned to a new alphabet,
With fingerings like a flame's equations—
People wondered why his out-of-tune guitar
Sang cerulean chords.

Trust me when I tell you, he was not the first man to listen
To Charley Patton, Son House, or Ike Z,
But he was the only man to listen to Julia Dodd's blues,
To open his arms and offer a throbbing vein.
He stroked his mama's hair like a fret board,
Combed out her blue notes,
Brushed out men's bourbon-breath promises,
Tied her hair back with guitar strings.

When a man has bad eyesight, he learns to play life by heart.
And Robert L.'s heart pumped
In the shine of his shoe or on the crease of his pants.
He knew the value of a plain lookin' woman and he knew
The danger of a pretty face.
He knew the blues of a man who just lost his woman,
But not the song of a bluesman framed in jealousy.
That was the scene his mama wouldn't talk about,
That forgotten lyric.

IV.
Had you entered the road house that night,
You would have heard ice cubes gossiping in drinks,
Men's hands rubbing women's thighs
Like brushes along cymbals,
Robert L.'s guitar,
Nervous and sweating.
You would have seen another man walking in his woman's shadow,
His cheeks pin-striped with tears.
You would have jumped at the crash of Sonny Boy's hand
Against the half-pint with the broken seal as it hit the woodplanked floor.
You would have heard Sonny's wisdom,

> "Man, don't never take a drink from an open bottle.
> You don't know what could be in it."

You might have heard the youth of Robert L.:

> "Man, don't never knock a bottle of whiskey from outta my hand."

You would have seen Robert's skin crease
As the poison from the next bottle sank
In, and the night separated into two:

> the crossroad leading to this bottle of death
> > or the path back to his mama's house.

V.
Why would a man who only dated homely women
Come to Three Forks, Mississippi, to date
The pretty wife of a jealous man?
This was not my idea.

Trust that this man was like a son to me,
That I hid in between his notes
And that it's difficult to recount the events;
It was painful to witness
Robert's weak eyes well with surprise,
Tears of women climbing through his pores,

His feet swelling through his shoes,
His blood looking for high ground,
I heard the gasp of men when the music stopped,
The drum roll of women's hearts,
I heard those Friday night chords
Floating into Mississippi air,
And the rain pounding on that tin-can roof
Like his mother's tears,
Washing over his bones.

The Absence of R.L. Burnside at New York's Autumn Blues Festival

Fife-and-drum music spires through the city
as Othar Turner comes down the aisle
of Symphony Space on Broadway
with his shoe-leather hands
fingering the wooden horn like a blind man
reading braille. And behind him,
Shimmy She Wobble-ing,
the new Gravel Strings band—
his progeny—plays traditional beats
on drums, surprisingly, not of wood.
Willie Foster wheels out on stage
with microphone and harmonica. He puts
the Mississippi saxophone to his lips
and breathes, what must be,
blue air in and out
between the chords of his hands
from a face I must have walked past
a million times downtown.

When they announce:
    We apologize for Burnside who was unable to be here tonight,

the man bearing bad news is wearing snakeskin boots.
    Figures, I say, fingering my Greyhound Bus
ticket back to D.C. and the change left from my last pay,
cursing Burnside and the boots,
till the alternate—the Little Dave Thompson Trio—
seizes the stage with collarless pastel suits
and playing electric guitars that wah-wah like newborn babies.
I see them embody through blue notes and smoke
with three instruments that sound like an orchestra.

    Damn, I didn't even wanna give them a chance,

I say, as I rock in my seat, forgetting the headline act,
wondering how Little Dave stole Satan's guitar pick.

"The Jungles Casino,"

They say, was a sharecropper's dream:
Nothin' formal about it.
After a handful of strokes, James P.—
With his thumbs thick as a fifth of whiskey—
Could still move from the far left
To the middle of the keyboard
As workboots stomped out his Charleston beat.
A day's work needed shakin' off, and this place
Was for a girl like her with washboard hands
And painted flat feet, or a boy like him
With sawdust under his nails and tree limbs
Growin' from the ends of his arms.
In this place where a woman's voice
Could teach men a new alphabet
Behind piano chords and laughter,
City boys would grunt through the door
With six-button-doublebreasted
Suits over their shoulders
And roach-killers on their feet,
But all the women would be taken
By the sweat-stained country boys
With city lights on their minds and cardboard
Stuck in the soles of their shoes, dancin'.

The Lifestory of Eddie James "Son" House Jr. as Told Through His Hands

In the fields, she touched me with dew-moist hands.
She was the earth lifted in my blue hands.

A man must live to have a life to sing.
He dies to have ashes lifted by hands.

Are there no limits to a bluesman's life?
Cotton & guitars: Picked by the same hands.

A train's whistle holds possibilities
Much like the backsides or the palms of hands.

In the audience, there are more blue eyes
Than I recall my hometown had black hands.

If you think these are wrinkles in my face,
Come, hear my life story told through my hands.

A preacher is nothing but a bluesman.
Bible? Guitar? All the same in my hands.

A workday is so long, the hours immense.
But my grip! Look at the size of these hands.

Your spirit becomes your eyes in prison.
Who questions a spirit with two strong hands.

Evie, with workdays as large as your eyes,
No one strums blues from my bones like your hands.

John Henry Tells Alan Lomax All About the Work Song The Night Before He Races the Steam Drill

1. *John, what is the work song?*

A man drops dead working 'long side you
and you raise his soul with your voice
the way a magician raises a body:
no strings attached.
Or blast your way into Big Ben Tunnel
with a hammer and spike
knowin' steel may be the only thing
standin' through dust and day.

A man must decide to lay his mind on a coolin' board
or a steel-strummed song.
You're college educated, tell me,
which would *you* choose?
You say hard work is all a man needs
to find success in America?
Get this down on your machine: That's a lie!
If a man has no home, no land of his own to work,
nothin' but wife and babies—
sometimes his only escape is his bottle or his work.
I don't drink, so I work;
ain't got nothin' to do with no dream
of my hands through Lady Liberty's hair.
This voice is a whole lot easier to raise than this hammer
so I sing, too. When you singin', it's like
that song has a pair of arms and it's helpin' you raise
the hammer; it holds the shakers' hands
like a father holds his child's.

2. *Is there some dream you're trying to fulfill by racing this steam drill?*

I can hammer a ten mile section in one day.
I can build everythin' that's ever been torn down
or the reverse. When a man is challenged
by machine, his shadow has a hard time
keepin' up with him.
Steam will never be a better worker than pride.
The crowd will stand on the side and ask,
did the sun beat him down
or kiss his backside? That glint
in the distance should be sweat on flesh
not some machine catchin' light.
Here's my dream: recognize me as a man.

3. *Other than the boss man, have any other white men come out here
to watch you?*

Irish men been drivin' steel
'long side me since I was old 'nough
to raise a hammer, but most white men
don't count 'em as white, because they work
as hard as a negro.
But if you don't count them,
from a distance,
with my hammer raised
over my bent back, a white man
once mistook me for a giraffe.
When the hammer came down
I told him this giraffe only takes cool sips
of steel under the sun's eye.
That's the game I play sometimes: I imagine
that man's watchin' me in the distance. The sky
is white hot behind me,
the ground ain't givin' nothin' back but dust,
my hammer comes down,
the sparks fly, and—for a second—the giraffe is dead.
Then he sees that it's all John Henry,
a natural man.

4. *Can you give me an authentic work song to record?*

Jinte on back there, give me some more.
Jinte hard now and let it roll.
Nod your head shorty—you almost out the door.

Jinte on down and put her on the floor.
Give it to me now and watch her stroll.
Jinte on back there, give me some more.

Now you don't want ole Sally to think you're a bore,
So Jinte on down there, tonight you gonna jelly roll.
Yeah, nod your head shorty, you almost out the door

On your way to the arms of a God fearin' whore.
Boy that gal sure gotta pretty little mole.
Jinte on back there give her some more.

Shake that rail sweet as a apple core.
Steel ain't nothin' but a woman, so give her some soul.
Nod its head shorty, you almost out the door.

Jinte on down boy, what you draggin' for?
Better git in there before they paddy roll.
Jinte on back there, give me some more.
Nod your head shorty—get on out that door.

5. *Is there anything you do at home to make a song like that come out of
you at work?*

What I do at home is my business.
Drivin' steel, linin' up equal signs from one end
of the Mississippi to the other, is my job.
The white man can't understand what the negro does in the light—
sun beating on my back as I spike a rail—
this alone baffles you. To study
what I do in the dark would destroy you.

This you may not understand:
A man climbs into a tunnel
at the top of day,
blackness becomes sunlight,
when he can't go no further,
when that hammer weighs twice as much as him
and all his bills and children put together,
someone lifts a voice and sings
that man's name, sings that man's song.

Or, you're three days away from camp,
a *death letter* comes telling you
your wife is dead or gone (same difference):
this is how a man learns to moan,
how to build himself
a heaven—a small one—
inside his own voice.

6. *What is it that keeps a man singing through the pain and the hard labor?*

Isn't it better for a man to die
buildin' somethin? I mean a man could die in a bar,
or in some woman's bed, or he could die as quietly as
a woman saying—for the last time—I love you,
in his own bed in the middle of the night,
but ain't nobody gonna sing no song about those men.
Naw, you gotta get out there and wrestle with the bears
of life and labor: the boss man, the bad men, the steam drills
that want to take your job. All those machines

against one man's voice.

Now, you just watch me.

Sharecroppers, Ring-Shouters and Stars

Stars are of little value
in the hands of a sharecropper.
It's the sun that dresses him in the morning,
the baptism of his throat with water
that gets him through the day,
the moon playing along the edges
of his wife's body
that brings him home at night.
At night, once a week, she leads him to the church;
they are God-fearing folks;
in the circle, their boots
shuffle spirit around the room:

The rhythm builds and

                   the rhythm breaks.

They "shout" in twos or

                   they "shout" in fours.

Their shoulders "hock";

                   the heads snap back.

The toes shuffle;

                   the heels stomp.

Off to the side

                   hands a'clappin'.

'Round the circle

                   hands like wind.

Shouter's spines

                   held straight.

Shouter's heels

                   swing the floor.

The faith in the circle

                   is the circle.

The spirit in their eyes

                   sings in their soles.

A woman shouts

                   from her knees;

her hair sweeps moonlight

                    from shouters' feet.
Then they sing:
                    "aaah, girl, go lowerer, lowerer."
She raises up:

                    shouters sing:
"rise from de mire, higherer, higherer"
                    and a fieldhand's shadow
springs from the floor.

A Young Woman's Blues

(Bessie Smith, b. April 15, 1894?— d. Sept. 26, 1937)

I. *Album*

The crowd's eyes betrayed you
Like your man's love.
   It's the story of any plain brown girl

Who falls in love with anyone
Who says, I love you.
   Your song, a mojo hand's magic,

Was no different from a woman who couldn't sing:
Your voice crept to a distant heart,
   But it never reached your own

Beneath emerald sequins and pastel eyeshadow.
That was the message I got from listening
   To your blue cry captured on disc.

Just as I thought all there was to know about a diva
Could be learned from her performance. . . .
   Off stage, the show went on as you

Stretched between men and women—
Some had their way with you and some
   You with them, backstage

Or on the other side of town—searching
Behind house lights and smiles
   For the applause.

II. *Stage*

With my headdress high and my dress cut low,
All the men know my name shining in lights
   And women wonder how I got my glow.

My man shoots straight and he's ready to fight.
Got a girl's number if he gets boring,
   And a fat fist if the money ain't right.

I don't play games; I ain't into scoring.
If you want a game playing woman, stop:
   Guard your heart! Don't call me till the morning.

I'll eat cheese until I get to the top.
I'm just a brown-faced girl who sings the blues—
   My one mistake: fell in love with a cop.

I hop the Yellow Dog, go where I choose.
What gets me through the night, can't be a sin:
   I got high-class taste and wear high-heel shoes.

See that lonesome road, Lord, you know it's gotta end,
I'm a good woman and I can get plenty men.

III. *Backstage*

Until Ruby Smith—your niece—ransacked the back room
Of your voice, your closet full of hats and heels,
   The delicate desires of your hands,

The ostrich—whose feathers draped
Over your shoulders—seemed the only one
   With something to hide.

Until the luster of life and no-good love
Slipped away like a last breath,
   Or the acoustic magic of your voice

Numb to liquor and lies,
And another woman's lingering perfume,
   The band—blowing,

Strumming, and beating behind you—
Looked hip to your next act
   And confident in their clothes.

What love was lodged in your heart, Bessie,
To hold in each fist,
   The power of a man's punch?

Betrayal was the last friend
To knock on your door
   With a smile pasted across her face.

Was that John G—your jealous man—
Or his mistress's shadow
   Creeping around the corner?

The fear of disappearing without a voice
Caused Ruby to tell
   Her best friend's secrets.

But it was *your* voice, Bessie,
That made the wine glasses shiver
   And the bow-legged men bow down.

It was the weakness of John,
Not his love, that kept him
   Close in bed at night.

Even with your trunk full of fine gowns—
With so many hanging onto your hem—small wonder
   They left you in a worn-yellow slip.

PART 3
PIANO FORTE

Undressing for Zora Neale Hurston

after Carl Phillips

Zora,
the sun over the fields
is telling a fable—
no lie—
about the honeybee that flew
over a garden of flowers
to land in a pile of shit,
about the fool in the sinking ship
who waited for a sign from God
to save him,
after God had already sent
the Coast Guard and thrown him a life jacket;
or as your Delia Jones would say,
It seems we don't never see goodness
right out; do we?
I'm remembering your fondness for folklore,
Zora, your desire for the truth in us,

and living for it.
In the bed, to the woman I don't love
enough, I am trying to say
that I need more than her apricot skin
and small toes, her hotcombed hair,
my hands at her wrists,
the forest between her legs—

that I need truth in my life
like a good folktale, a blues song,
a chord from a steel guitar,
something like music . . .

Zora, Zora,
the sun is fingering through
underwear and books; socks and CDs;
the random order of this room; my eyes,

where I left them on the night stand.
I am wondering about
sweat and crossroads,
unfinished stories,
hats and feathers,
lies and jokes,
traveling alone, arriving home,
and the size of my skull
in your hands.

Zora, this morning,
hungry again, I lay naked,
just dreaming, dreaming...
I watched my body move
between dialects and regions
and I had forgotten the particulars;
yours was the only face I could make out;
I could see that our journey had been long;
your eyes were filled with new truths. You
stood barefoot on my bare feet and we didn't say
nothin', not a word, we looked each other
straight in the eye and we danced, Zora, we danced.

The Notes That Fall at the End of Lines

You gotta listen
As words drift between words.
It's like the falling harmonics

Of the strummed-chord answer

To a young French reporter's question
Posed to Monk:
    What kind of music
    Do you like to listen to
    Other than jazz?
    When Monk says, *I like all kinds of*
    Good music,
    The young man asks, *What about*
    Country? Classical?
    Monk turns to his drummer,

    Says, *He must be hard of hearing,*

Not as the words are spoken
But as they disappear.

It's not the music as it plucks
Your eardrum that causes your head
To bop
On the question
Of Jazz,

But the downbeat
On its way to the part of your brain
That doesn't ask.

What Does It Mean When a Man Dreams of Lingerie?

Why would I march through Victoria's Secret
trying to look like a man
if it weren't true
that I do feel comfortable among
push-up bras and crotchless panties,
lace garters and strap-up brassieres,
that I do dream of decorating
my décolleté? But, it's clear
there's nothing this powerful
in a man's arsenal of seduction.

My holding midnight blue
camisoles up to my chest
in a mirror brags
boldness and sensitivity,
the hologram of love.

What does it all mean,
my standing here holding
undergarments, shadows
of my former lover,
but not her body?

The philosopher, Richard Pryor,
once said of black love
that a couple either fucks or fights;
there is no in between.
I realize I'm getting too old
for the contrasts of love,
when a vibrato comes from behind
a rack of satin robes.
Cumbia music floats
over the heads
of souls shopping for happiness.
I follow rhythms through delicate
textiles to find a man,

his face peering back
through a pair of ass-out
pantyhose, his face
where the ass should be.
He's tall but stout,
like a contra bass. Mingus?
I inquire.

Look at this body stockin' boy.
You see this labyrinth of lace, intricacy,
clear, opaque,
chaos in structure;
that's our lives.
We're just down here vibrating.
Men and women are like
a duet of a drum set
and a bass
that don't talk to each other.
They don't love anymore
because they don't talk anymore.
A man can play the hell outta a woman,
be all over her like a horn,
but he won't know her like his horn;
that's why they can't make music.
You gotta love her
from her fresh hair to her dirty panties.

A vein in my neck throbs.
I say, To hell with you, Mingus.

His left hand palms my head
like a fret board;
his right hand bows
a razor over my right eye,
deeply, andante.
Light hemorrhages out.

There, he says, you have to see
differently with a woman;
talk to her not like she's a man,

sometimes. Switch up.
You know, I used to play
avant-garde bass
when nobody else did;
now I play 4/4 because
none of the other players do.
Sometimes, it's cold blooded like that.
Sometimes your woman is trapped
beneath the vibrato
of the strings, man;
sometimes you gotta pull her
in close and strum her
in her sleep, sometimes
soft, sometimes loud,
piano forte, like music
that's about the living
and the dead, or a pair
of shaved brown legs
in sheer black hose, forever,
walking out of your life.

Two Drunks with Different Approaches to Life

after Oscar Brown Jr.

A disco ball hangs from the ceiling;
The silver carcass casts a constellation of asterisks,
Which dance over bass drums and lies.

A good customer sticks
Two fingers in his mouth,
But still he's too limp to raise a wolf whistle
For the ladies livid with laughter as they
Float past him wrapped in shawls of smoke.
As he blows, his head strobes in a heave of hot air.
His conversation is moist.
Divorce and whiskey, icons of the depressed,
Mingle on his breath.
Barroom regulars place him in a lower class:
>   *The last thing a man needs,*
>   *when he needs a drink,*
>   *is a drink.*
Another man measures his sorrow in sips.
Money problems dilute in his beer.
He's all elbows and knees on the dance floor.
The sad man faces down at the bar,
But looks up catching the eyes
Of a couple at a table, and he sings:

>   *My story begins not too long ago, in bedder days*
>   *When my in-laws said, even with money, I had bedder ways*
>   *You wanna hear how far a God fearin' man can sink?*

>   *Somebody buy me a drink.*

His eyes roll staccato;
His head, an off-beat metronome,
And then, again, with more authority now, he sings:

>   *It doesn't take looong for a good man to break*
>   *The weight of a glaaass is heavier than mos' think*

I threw love away for a whoe house and a clink

Dammit! I said, somebody buy me a drink!

The one who sips, has had enough:
He takes deliberate steps outside,
Under wails and whispers from automobiles,
Ignores cry-for-help hands and
Lips that have not been tasted,
Passes the headlines of tomorrow's paper,
And dissolves into the night, whistling.

Silent Partner

The Duke treated him, in the 40s,
Like one of his women:
Paid his rent, even bought his clothes.
Folks thought his glass-in-hand,
Smoke-a-pack-a-day life
Would be enough for a finale.
Thought some god
Had climbed past his infant smile
And down his brass horn throat
With a sack of cancer. But nothing
Of spirit or flesh or straight or gay
Could kill the sound of his piano
Waving white-key flags
Under his blurred black-finger attack.

The 50s brought the coda:
Audiences bubbled from the sound
Of this invisible grace-note of a man.
Marquees were parents with good news:

> *The Savoy presents*
> ** Billy Strayhorn **
> *Accompanied by Duke Ellington*
> *& His Orchestra.*

His story reads like that moment
Before the conductor raises his hands
For the downbeat. When the room
Falls silent and ears brace to fill
With flats and sharps.
Like the silence of the Duke's
Shadow when his arms are flailing
On the bandstand, or when his partner—
Billy Strayhorn—composed
Heatedly under his shade.

J.J. Johnson Changes Tempo

When J.J. raises his horn to his lips,
the loss of Vivian laces each note.
He holds that slide like
it's her hand
and moonbeams burrow
through smoke-filled rooms,
a hundred legs dance on brass shimmers,
a thousand snap dragons swallow low notes.

While other cats rush
in blaring through the cursive bore, J.J.,
smooth as long shaved legs,
whispers through its hollow body.

If he plays with an open bell,
every smile has a gold tooth.
If he uses a mute,
men sob into calloused hands.

But when Vivian was at his side,
when the tempo rang like an eighth note
chain gang, when jealous lovers reached for razors
and hired guns pulled up chairs,
even J.J.'s whisper,
which filled men's lungs like a deep kiss,
and wrapped women in two strong arms,
could only be explained by his slide
trombone fluttering like a satyr's tongue.

Voodoo

for E. Ethelbert Miller

Once, I showed Ethelbert
A love poem
I wrote about a woman
I was dating.

What you think, man?
I asked.

His comments were an X
He drew from one end
To the other.

Then he folded it up.
Gave it back to me.

Man, don't you know,
I broke up
With that woman.

How Does a Man Write a Poem

at midnight? What better light
to write by than a woman's body
filled with her spirit and her mother's wit?

That body—which does to his words
what the moon does to the night—
is a song that plays

freely in that part of the mind
that makes a man hum, or whistle—
when he least expects it—

a tune that sticks to him for life.
Tonight, the song is a request:
Write me a poem, please.

But what is left to write,
when the poem is curled up next to him in bed,
her hair hanging over his chest,

a willow breathing in his ear?
Although no money is wagered on his answer,
no love lost—

she's never told him she loves him—
he still weighs the odds of her joy;
of her loss:
He picks up the pen.

PART 4

RISE

The Journey of Henry "Box" Brown

Perhaps Henry Brown remembered Golgotha,
the taunt of the trail, the inevitable end—
the enviable end—the sting of vinegar doused eyes,
much like his own urine drenched skin, or
he remembered those who pined in bondage,
those who longed for the freedom of either his box,
the carpenter's geometric womb, the nails
pulled straight from hands to hold
the walls together till his new life,
or the voice, as if from above, in his head
which whispered, "Go and get a box,
and put yourself in it," that voice which dreamt
him through white hands, through bounds
his black face could not cross; first,
to the express office, the box placed on its end,
so he started with his head downwards—
as if he were on the verge of life—
the crate marked "This Side Up
With Care," but no one cared and no one
bent to break his falls or to stop the blood
from rushing to his temple—
two hours on his head, veins strained, eyes
bulged, death's breath held—
then, three o'clock in the morning, a depot,
now with the box directed right side up,
to the home of a friend in Philadelphia
whose trembling voice—imagine,
on the outside and his voice trembled—
asked, *Is all right within?* to which Henry,
in a trumpeted tone, replied, *All right.*

Sharecropper's Emancipation

Sometimes when Boss man smile
And talk in my face,
I can see fields of Colored people
Pickin' white teeth
Like bolls of cotton.

Monochord

Hedley: One string make plenty, plenty music.
            —*from August Wilson's Seven Guitars*

Before guitar and fiddle
were plucked by griot
fingers and thumb,
before one note
from Gabriel's trumpet,
before one apple passed
between two lovers,
or the *one* of a first kiss,
or the glance before the kiss,
or the last word before she says,
Goodbye— forever—a one string
between distant lovers
used to bring hearts together;

but now, I ask the one
string of her concentric navel,
of the plume of our incense,
of fire above the candle
next to where we lie, the one
shimmer outside my window
where a raindrop falls on a branch
under the moon, hanging
a star on a tree, I ask the one
unfaithful act, which destroyed
the trust, the one
strand of her hair
found in my bed, one night
of forgiveness, of our God,
of her leg in a split skirt,
of the zipper of her dress,
of the sound of her voice
in the dark, of her scent
in my memory, the one
string of her spine, of the water
running for her bath,

of her mercury arms,
of ovum and sperm,
of ink spelling her name,
one string outlining her silhouette, or
of the shoe she's left here, small,
empty as my eyes, of this one
string strummed in remembrance,
with the sincerity of history,
now that my woman has gone,
where is the beauty of folklore?

Kind of Blue

How I tried to explain
the love I heard between
the notes, how I reached
for you when he played,
how when a man's heart splits open
in the middle of a song—
whether playing or just connecting—
it is not unlike a gasp
for air, at the close of sex,
at that moment, how wondrous
our faces seem when we hear
a soul speak through a horn,
how perfect the grammar
between the notes.

And it was not because I knew
I would leave you years later,
in D.C.— once I found you
in bed with another man—
that I took you downtown
to see Miles Davis in concert
at Cincinnati's Music Hall;
it was just because you could leave me
and I knew—even then when I knew
nothing, when I had just bought
my first Miles Davis album—
I knew that good memories haunt us
as much as the bad ones.
And that night in '85
I think it was because I loved
him that you hated Miles Davis.
Oh, you wore that short skirt—
your legs pouring out
like two high Cs from a trumpet's bell—
but you still had an attitude.
You said he was a heroin addict,
a junkie, that his skin stretched

like leather because of drugs.
And I was reminded
of my neighbor who was on crack
and the night he came to beg for some money,
this guy who had a wife and two kids,
I asked him why he got high,
as if it were my business.
With his head turned from me he said,
Man, it's like you're havin' sex
and you come and you just keep
comin' and comin', 15 to 20 minutes straight
And then he looked at me and asked
Have you ever known love like that?
I gave him five dollars that night.

And despite your rolling eyes,
and the Tsssst you made with your teeth,
I bought you a ticket to the concert.

Remember how we sat on the front row
and how, in the middle of the first set,
Miles walked across the stage
on that tightrope invisible
to all but him, how he stopped at its edge,
and how he played "Time After Time"
and broke it down to you
and stared first at your legs
and then straight into your eyes.
I wasn't jealous, you see,
because he made my point for me.
And to this day, because of that night,
I know for certain
that you still love one of us.
And look at you now, years later,
getting high in your apartment,
your stereo spinning a Miles Davis disc.
You no longer question
what kind of blue pulls a man's skin
so tightly over the face.
Yes. What do the uninitiated, who can only listen,
know about this kind of love?

Would You Like Your Fortune Told?

You say *hold my hand* while you read
my fortune in the *New York Daily News,*
that the headline—

   Scientists Predict Doomsday—
actually, has nothing to do with me,
that the key to my love life lies

in the off-track betting page,
that my career path awaits in the mysteries
of today's lottery numbers. . . .

You say it's a gift, intuition
from God; the newspaper, a mere tool;
you could predict my future with anything,

an *Essence* magazine or a Nerf football.
I hear that *You got sight* and curiosity
has made me a believer.

Carry me through today's news
in your brown, gracile hand; this touch,
mine placed in yours,

is more mystical than the prediction.
Be as gentle as you were with the single
mother who had no money,

just eyes like silver pieces that fell
into your palms with the hope of a tither,
with the need of a woman who learned—

through love that's gone wrong—
the definition of faith.
I can see the woman approach you

with her kids in tow. . . .
It was not from this New York world,
your telling her fortune for free,

the two of you, strangers,
holding each other. After I give
you my hand, how do I continue

to believe what I read in the papers?

To My Brothers

for Cordell and Ken

Men spend their whole lives focusing their vision.
Blessings only come through the freedom of vision.

What is said of the man who fails in life?
Is it possible that he too had vision?

What is more immaculate than a wealthy woman's toes,
Or a poor woman's faith? Her immense vision?

A man without a woman knows the longing of love
As a man without money knows the salve of vision.

Job lost family and land—his body covered with destruction—
But nothing can destroy a prayer with vision.

Man born of a woman is said to be damned;
Truth, this gives man his first taste of vision.

Paint the walls of my house black!
I want room to open my eyes and set free my vision.

Aaron, you will always be your brother's brother;
A man's reach should never surpass this in his vision.

The Overcoat

is not what I remember,
not how I felt in it, my first taste
of being *clean,* as my brothers put it,

put in a way that a ten-year-old
could understand;
but what I remember now

is the emptiness of the coat,
not the sure cherub effect of me
in an ankle-length, maroon, velour

overcoat with a black, faux-leather collar.
No. What I remember
is all of this not being enough to prevent

suspicion of shoplifting
on a lazy stroll through a shopping plaza,
in Cuyahoga Falls, Ohio, a suburb

we blacks in town called Caucasian Falls.
I get confused by guns; they erase memory.
You don't remember eyes of adults

who thought better of you. Any of those memories
rub against a blue uniform, handcuffs, billyclubs.
It's years later before I remember

a white man, just a few weeks before
my window-shopping excursion,
in another mall, on another day, telling me

he could see Jesus in my small face.
If I had remembered his words
then, looking down the barrel

of that gun, I would have thought
he had just set me up. Just another face
with words, another lie. . . .

I look at all three feet of the coat,
lackluster now in my hands,
and wonder what would make four

cops pull guns on my brother and me,
both of us well-dressed and polite
and not much bigger than our coats.

Please, don't tell me the one about
them just doing their jobs, that we looked
like we may have been concealing weapons

in our Robert Hall mark-downs.
Could they have had, instead of surveillance,
time-lapse photography cameras in the stores?

Could they see that we
were two boys with hope growing
in our hearts like tumors, that we

would have grown into two men
who would have thought life for us
would never be so close to death

on the wrong side of town,
so vivid, like these worn spots on the coat
singed bald by age, empty as bullet holes?

Maybe not. Maybe I have said   nothing.
Maybe this is a story you hear every day
and I have nothing to report—

no bruises or death or visible pain.
Like I said, I barely remember the coat,
the faces of the cops,

or what my mother said
when she came to pick us up
and found us surrounded;

you see, if I remember,
if I make it something to hold onto,
instead of a blurry dream,

they win. My life repeats itself
every time death shakes her finger
in my face and I walk away.

It's not that I don't believe death
can come so close and miss every time,
but I recognize the blessing:

I know what it means
to stand here today and tell you
what it feels like when a white hand reaches

into my pockets—hoping for drugs
or any excuse they can find—and pulls out
the relief of nothingness.

Rise

"For there they that carried us away captive required of us a song. . . . "
PSALMS 137:3

I. *Field Holler*

Dead man, we need water now in the fields
to wash this fist from our throats so we can
sing sunshine into our hands and feet. Now,
while our morning is still dark and purple,
bring water. We need the art of droplets
on tree bark and leaves, after the storm cries
over our heads. Weeds grow around honey-
suckle and cotton and our fingers free
their chains. Whose touch will free us—hearts
stiffened, mouths dry from song, feet thick with clay—
from our weeds? Our mules are tired of plowing
through our footsteps. The soil has lost her taste
for our sweat. And through the night, the moon hangs
on its chain while our tears learn sleep's sweetness.

On its chain, while our tears learn sleep's sweetness,
the harvest moon dances through the night, but
only to one song: it hears the echo
of our footsteps as they lead to the field,
the hollow reeds of our spines as we lift
our heads toward home. We will welcome morning:

His clothes is full of patches,
His hat is full of holes,
Stoopin' down pickin' cotton
From off the bottom holl
Po far-mer, po—far-mer,
    Po farmer,
They get all the farmer make

And tomorrow, after the sun's whip rests,
our bloody clothes will be left to explain.

II. *Prison Camp Work Song*

Our bloody clothes'll be left to explain
why pickaxes and hammers sing to stone.
Crime—wastin' our voices on rocks and guards,
watchin' sparrows dance just below clouds, while
Alberta's face shimmies beneath my eyelids.
Workin' without pay makes the days go slow
And the nights be counted in minutes.

Now give me water, Lord, when I'm thirsty (hunh!)
Honey, give me whiskey when I'm dry (hunh!)

When Boss Man hears us singin' he knows
we's breakin' rocks into hand-held stars, he
forgets the team's slow man. I'm the first man,
ahead of younger men come mornin', been
first man in my team for 15 years now.

III. *Chain Gang*

Yeah, first man in my team for *fif-teen* years now—
that's convict years, no woman, no drink, just
work—so a man's gotta learn him some songs
to keep his head. Guards don't guard a singin' man.
A gun? A knife? They're no match for my song.
I just lullaby 'em till they lean back
with their mouth open like catfish and—
for those few minutes—I'm free. I just pour
the emotion I would've poured into
a woman into a song, it's easy:

Now give me water, Lord, when I'm thirsty (hunh!)
Honey, give me whiskey when I'm dry (hunh!)
Give me Alberta, when I need her (hunh!)
And heaven when I die. (hunh!)

IV. *Levee Camp Moan*

And heaven when I die. Oh Lord, I say, heaven when I die,
that's when I'll straighten up this back.
Stars will just be holes peeking through the black
'cause the dark will be the light and the moon will have to sigh.

At least I'll be out of here before Mr. Cholly starts to cry.

I've met with ups and downs of life and better days I've saw
But I never knew what mis'ry was till I came to Arkansas.

And if I go to hell, compared to this, it'll be cooler if I fry.

I'll drink hot water and eat spiced shrimps with the devil.
Slide my steel guitar and stomp a red foot in dirt.
Learn me some new songs 'bout old days on the levee
and none of 'em will be to the rhythm of this dusty, old shovel.
They's got women in hell and I'll find time to flirt
cause I'll be too far down to dig and my worries won't be so heavy.

V. *Log Rollers*

Too far down to dig a hole and my worries ain't as heavy,
'cause now we ain't got to move them logs by hand:
four men to a side? that's eight hearts beatin' like a band.
Oh, it took a heap of work to clear a way on this Delta Levee.

The more we'd yell "bow and come" the more they'd fall, one and ev'ry.
But they kept a rollin', so if we couldn't move 'em we'd strap on the
    "bull band":
a harness strap over the shoulders with a liftin' pole fitted for our hands.
Bow and Come! Keep it Moving! You'd hear and see logs a rollin' by
    the bevy.

We'd sing: *Gimme another partner (hunh!)*
            Give him to me quick (hunh!)
            I need another hand (hunh!)
            On the end of this here stick (hunh!)

By evenin',
        there was plenty food and fife-and-drum so men wouldn't wander.
Yeah, we had us a time, but not much money for a workin' man to squander.

VI. *Plow Men*

Yeah, not much money for a workin' man to squander
with a acre to split 'mongst a team of men
we'd be singin to keep our minds off sin.
Plowin' the soil while women chopped cotton up yonder

all spring. Looking back at that work, we men of the hoe
fed every mouth raised up from the dust.
Did the hoein' and plowin' without raisin' a fuss—
keepin' food on the table even when the crops were slow.

We didn't much care whether it was cotton, yam or millet
but a dry spell, boy, now that could bring a scare.
It'd take more than a crop of singers
to calm a dry field. You see strong men cryin', can't help but to feel it.
During most of the year, plowmen of the South were there
between cotton rows with a sack and a song, a hymn or a tractor.

VII. *That Old Time Religion*

Whether stretchin' between rows of cotton with a hymn or a tractor,
or clappin' hands and gettin' happy with Jesus in our hearts,
we be stompin' our feet and plowin', souls singin' *John the Revelator*—
that's the disciple who told the truth from the start.

He said, *God called Adam by his name (hunh!)*
       but ole Adam refused to answer, (hunh!)
       he was naked and ashamed.
And that's why now we livin' under man's laws.

Nowadays, your own mother will talk about you
whether she's in church or thinnin' whiskey at a bar
and the preacher might wink at your wife, too.
So when you take that Christ walk, boy,
                     you better be willin' to step far

'Cause you can be in the pulpit jumpin' up and down
but jokers still be out on the corner yellin', *Alabama Bound!*

VIII. *Blues*

Jokers standin on the comer yellin' Alabama Bound!
I say that's me standin on the corner yellin' Alabama Bound!
But I stopped actin' a fool 'cause I heard a soft-laced sound.

Sister girl jumped up and began to shout.
I say sister jumped and then began to shout.
She said, Yep, I'm sho glad that corn liquor's runnin' out.

But when that Yellow Dog come a callin'.
You know when that Yellow Dog starts to callin'.
Her wig will be tilted and her heels won't be stallin'.

And a yelp won't be heard from a hound in heat.
Not a yelp will be heard from a hound in heat.
'Cause only losin' a good woman can put a fool in his seat.

The blues will wear a man down like a cold-blooded disease.
Just like everybody you be lovin' be so gotdamned hard to please.

IX. *Chicago*

Everybody you be lovin' be so gotdamned hard to please
especially these city gals with hemlines way above their knees.

I'm just a country boy, but I got big city dreams
and Chitown's the place where Mississippi waters flow.
City boys may not like it, but it's the sanctified truth:
slide guitars and harmonicas ain't no city-like machines.

You smell that pot o' chitlins and that kettle of greens?
Can't raise hogs on the south side and crops don't come from the street.
Hell yeah, I miss home, but I'm here with purpose:
I wanna high-society woman who drives her own Cadillac

and it takes a mule-drivin' man to put her on her back.
Boy, I miss my mama and sisters and the girls from church,
even knock-kneed girlfriends with big, flat feet. There's no shame,
makin' it in the big city, when you got good game.

X. *Big Band*

You livin' in the big city; you got good game.
You just got to the big city, and you say you got game?
Then blow that horn, boy, and earn your fame.

City lights are high Cs from a trumpet's bell.
City lights shine brightest on payday nights.
City lights are mere sequins on a woman's gown.

Trombones don't take no for an answer.
Them trombones don't take nos for answers.
They only make that growl for big-legged dancers.

City lights make men leave they daddy's house.
City lights make young girls sell, what men never own.
City lights make fools out of hipsters.

The sax wails; the piano rolls; a freedom dance, the big band brings
for the man with no money to spend, and no life to sing.

XI. Jazz: Take 1

But to the man with money to spend and a life to sing—
what can you tell *him* that he doesn't already know?
That the A train doesn't always lead to Harlem?
That a quart of milk will cost you a day's wage?

What do you call the music that rings in your head when your woman
calls out another man's name? Yeah, can you play some of *that* for me?
Can you make a song out of my day at work? And what
was the name of the last man who looked you in the eye

when he shook your hand; made you a promise he knew
he couldn't keep? Is it true that a mockingbird
can sing heartache and bebop? Would you know
an organ chord from a crying mother?

Is the comfort the same: in the arms of a man
and the lingering gaze from a woman?

XII. Jazz: Take 2

Can the lingering gaze of a woman
have more strength than the arms of a man?

Did Ellington compose *Diminuendo and Crescendo in Blue*
from a mother's joy and wails? Have you ever heard a black man
sing heartache and bebop both through a smile? When
you become a man, will you understand why a father's

reach is not always equal to the love under his sweat?
Hear that bass drum, men building
a country with two sticks and a nervous foot? Have you reckoned
Mingus—*Pithecanthropus Erectus?*

Is milk always sweeter straight from the breast?
Is it true: Harlem is getting smaller and the city is getting larger?
Could an ostrich fly
if he spent more time being real?

XIII. *Liner Notes*

To spend more time being real
Refer to J.J. Johnson's Columbia Legacy years.

Wrong notes become bridges; a word, recitative
and the sound can fill an opera house. Even
as the note is struck in a Delta jook joint at midnight

a brushstroke inspires a sunrise jam session
in Paris. But that's just the sound. *A Song*
For My Father plays for mothers in London to buy

high heels to at Harrods. Like a spirit walker, one note
plucked from a modal chord continues
on its journey not to descend, there's no coming down,

not to ascend—no difference: a ballerina's *jeté*.
a boy's Lindyhop—but to hear, before the song,

> *dead men*

clear their throats to water fields with voices.

Note: Traditional lyrics in "Rise" quoted from The Library of Congress' Alan Lomax Collection.